This Book Belongs To:

Made in the USA
Monee, IL
04 August 2022

10954748R00066